P9-DFQ-517

Prehistoric Mammals

CONTENTS

© Aladdin Books Ltd

Designed and produced by
Aladdin Books Ltd
70 Old Compton Street
London W1

All rights reserved

Printed in Belgium

First published in the
United States in 1985 by
Gloucester Press
387 Park Avenue South
New York NY 10016

ISBN 0-531-17001-2

Library of Congress Catalog
Card No. 84-62468

Certain illustrations have previously appeared in the "A Closer Look
At" series published by Gloucester Press.

A CLOSER LOOK AT

Prehistoric Mammals

ELIZABETH STRACHAN

Illustrated by
PETER BARRETT, GIOVANNI CASELLI AND RICHARD ORR

Consultant
JOYCE POPE

Gloucester Press
New York · Toronto · 1985

Animal Types

All the animals on Earth can be grouped according to special characteristics that they share. For example, all animals with an internal bony skeleton are grouped as vertebrates. Those with a hard outer skeleton, or none at all – insects, worms and jellyfish, for example – are invertebrates.

Within the vertebrates are smaller groups – fish, birds, reptiles, amphibians and mammals. As the chart below shows, each of these groups has special characteristics of its own. The first vertebrate animals to live on land were amphibians, able to breathe oxygen from both the air and from water, just as can the frogs and newts of today. From these first amphibians, the reptiles, mammals and birds arose.

	Fish are cold-blooded and breathe through their gills. Their eggs are laid, or spawned, in water.
	Amphibians are cold-blooded and breathe through both lungs and gills. They can live on land or in water.
	Reptiles are cold-blooded and breathe through lungs. Their young are hatched from eggs.
	Birds are warm-blooded, kept warm by their feathers. Their young are hatched from eggs.

What is a mammal?

The basic characteristic of mammals is that their young are fed on milk from their mother for the first weeks or months after birth. This milk is produced by the mother from special glands inside her body. This means that young mammals are cared for more fully than young fish and reptiles.

Mammals are warm-blooded, which means that their bodies stay at nearly constant temperatures. Their fur or hair helps keep them warm, and sweat glands help them cool down. Mammal brains are larger in proportion to their bodies than those of other animals, so they are more intelligent and better able to make the most of their environment in some situations.

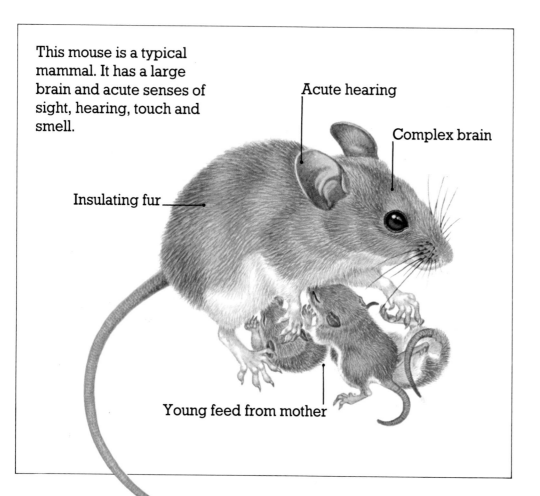

This mouse is a typical mammal. It has a large brain and acute senses of sight, hearing, touch and smell.

Acute hearing

Complex brain

Insulating fur

Young feed from mother

Life on Earth

The Earth is a living planet, populated by hundreds of thousands of different types of plants and animals. Living things have made their home in the coldest ocean and in the hottest desert. Even the air we breathe is full of tiny organisms. This abundance of life began in the Earth's oceans, over 3,000 million years ago. It wasn't until about 350 million years ago that animals first ventured onto land. From fossils preserved in rocks, geologists can piece together how the story of life unfolded, as animals changed with the changing conditions on Earth.

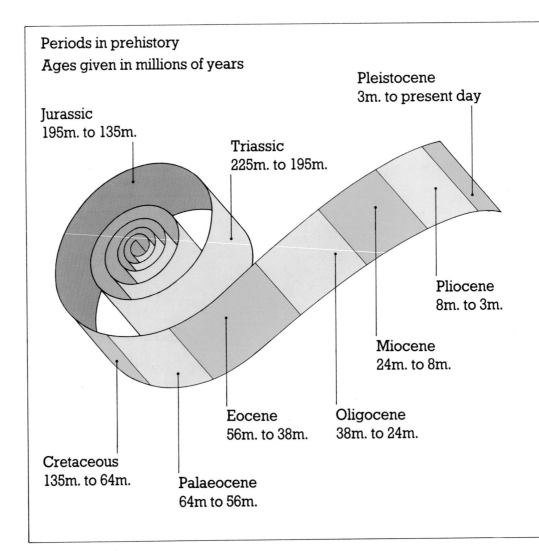

Periods in prehistory
Ages given in millions of years

Pleistocene
3m. to present day

Jurassic
195m. to 135m.

Triassic
225m. to 195m.

Pliocene
8m. to 3m.

Miocene
24m. to 8m.

Eocene
56m. to 38m.

Oligocene
38m. to 24m.

Cretaceous
135m. to 64m.

Palaeocene
64m to 56m.

Finding out about the past

Geologists give names to the different periods of the Earth's history. From the age of the rocks, the age of fossils contained within them can be determined. For example, the bones of Arsinotherium – a distant relative of the elephant – were found in rocks dating from 30 million years ago. This places it in the Oligocene period. Fossils from deeper and older layers of rocks, are of animals from even earlier in the Earth's history.

This Arsinotherium skeleton was gradually covered by river sands which hardened to form layers of rock. Movements of the Earth and erosion eventually exposed the fossil for geologists to find.

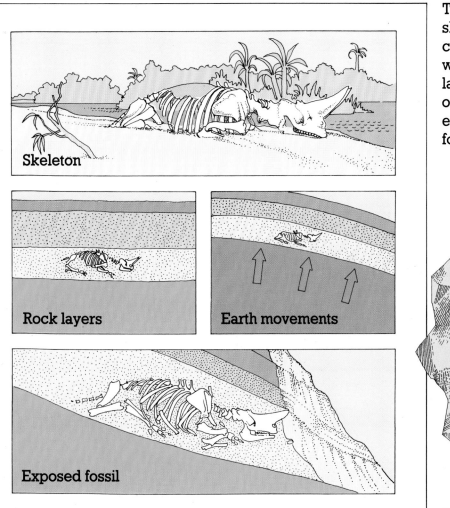

Skeleton

Rock layers

Earth movements

Exposed fossil

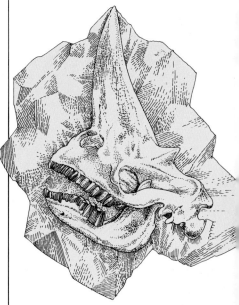

Fossil skull of Arsinotherium

Early Ancestors

Among the first land animals known from fossil records were a group of mammal-like reptiles. These lived about 300 million years ago. Originally, they had a squat, sprawling posture, their limbs sticking out sideways rather like those of a modern-day crocodile.

Gradually, their limbs grew longer and were held under the body, enabling them to move more quickly. Some had teeth suitable for stabbing and tearing flesh. Others were plant-eaters, with teeth that could grind and chew tough vegetation.

Cynognathus

Thrinaxodon

Survival and change

These changes took place over thousands of years, through a process known as natural selection. Individual animals of the same species vary slightly from one another – as in any litter of kittens. Some variations make it more difficult for the individual to survive in the wild – an all white coat, for example, is easily spotted by predators. These animals will tend not to survive.

Other variations help in the struggle for life, and individuals with these will be more likely to breed and pass on their characteristics to their offspring. Some of these early animals developed to become the first true mammals.

These early creatures survived for almost 70 million years. Cynognathus and Thrinaxodon had mammal-like features.

Kannemeyeria

Euparkeria

The Age of the Dinosaurs

The Age of the Dinosaurs began about 225 million years ago and lasted for 140 million years. Throughout this period, the dinosaurs were the dominant group of land animals. There were huge carnivores, such as Tyrannosaurus rex, and giant herbivores which lived in herds. But alongside them, the mammals also flourished.

Their warm blood and protective fur allowed them to be active during the cool of night, while the many dinosaurs were inactive. These mammals were small, shrewlike creatures, feeding on insects, reptile eggs and fruits. Some were ground-dwellers, like the protolungates. Others, such as Erythrotherium, adapted to life in the trees, and were the ancestors of the lemurs, apes and monkeys of today.

Protolungate

Erythrotherium

Tyrannosaurus rex

The Rise of the Mammals

Dramatically and mysteriously, about 64 million years ago, the dinosaurs died out. Smaller reptiles such as snakes, lizards and crocodiles survived. So did the birds, which had developed from the dinosaurs, but the giant ones disappeared forever. No one knows why this happened, but from that time onward, the world was left to the mammals.

They came out to feed during the day as well as the night. Some were herbivores, others preyed on small reptiles and other mammals. Among the animals of this period were early relatives of shrews, moles, rodents and carnivores such as dogs, each exploiting the new opportunities for food.

Protictis

Taeniolabus

Plesiadapis

Planetetherium

13

Prey and Predators

During the Eocene period, which began about 56 million years ago and lasted 18 million years, different mammals specialized in different ways of life. Uintatherium, for example, was a plant-eater the size of a modern rhinoceros and probably lived in very much the same way. Coryphodon was another herbivore, similar in size and shape to the hippopotamus.

Early meat-eaters

Feeding on the herbivores, and scavenging on the carcasses of dead animals were the carnivores. One of the largest of these was Patriofelis, about the size of a small bear. Fossils of Patriofelis have been found in North America, Europe and Asia.

Perhaps the most extraordinary carnivore of this period was the giant flightless bird, Diatryma. Diatryma was over 3m (9.8 ft) tall and had a head the size of a modern pony. It is shown here attacking a group of Hyracotherium. Hyracotherium was no larger than a rabbit, but was the ancestor of the modern horse.

Hyracotherium

Coryphodon

atriofelis

Diatryma had powerful long legs and probably ran faster than the carnivorous mammals.

Diatryma

Uintatherium

R. ORR

15

Success and Failure

The Eocene period was followed by the Oligocene, which lasted until about 24 million years ago. The mammals of this period were closer relatives to those living today. Many types of ancestral antelopes and horses flourished, and predators became more specialized.

Cats and dogs

During the Oligocene period, the first saber-toothed cats appeared. Some scientists think that the two huge, dagger-like upper teeth were used to stab into the hides of such prey as the large plant-eaters. They would then bleed to death through their wounds. Others think that the teeth were used like knives, to slice up the carcasses of animals already dead. Other cats had biting jaws with razor-sharp teeth, like the lions and tigers of today, leaping on their prey and severing the backbone at the neck. These in the end proved most successful and survived.

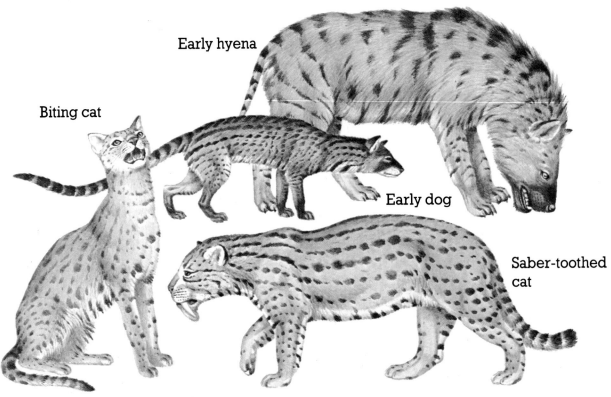

Early hyena

Biting cat

Early dog

Saber-toothed cat

Doomed giants

Paraceratherium, shown here, was probably the largest land mammal that ever lived, standing over 5m (16·5ft) tall at the shoulder. It probably fed on high vegetation in open woodlands, as does the giraffe.

Paraceratherium

The Spread of the Grasslands

This scene is from the Miocene age, which began about 24 million years ago. The Earth's climate had become gradually drier. The thickly forested areas of earlier times began to give way to open grasslands, and the mammals accordingly adapted to these new environments.

Herds and packs

Many of the herbivores lived in herds. This gave them greater protection from their predators, though old, injured or sick individuals were still likely to be captured. Some carnivores, such as the ancestors of today's hunting dogs, also found advantage in numbers. They hunted in packs, the dominant animals acting as leaders.

Trilophodon

Moropus

Gazelles

The larger grassland animals

Among the larger animals that roamed the grasslands was the Deinotherium, a relative of the elephant, with tusks and an elongated trunk used to gather food. Another was Trilophodon, with a short trunk and elongated lower jaw. Moropus – related to the horse – had large clawed feet, which may have been used for digging up roots.

The adaptable ape

Proconsul, the ape in the foreground of the illustration, was spread widely over the plains of Africa. Helpless on its own, it lived in groups and its superior intelligence enabled it to exploit its environment and survive.

Deinotherium

Proconsul

Mammals in Isolation

Over the ages, it was not just the Earth's climate that changed. The Earth's continents moved, some splitting up from larger land masses and later joining others. At one time South America formed a single continent with Africa. Later it became separate, eventually linking up with North America, which had split off and drifted away from Europe.

These movements of the continents affected the lives of the mammals living on them. Isolated, they could develop in unique ways, but when the continents became joined, other animals moved in and competed for the limited food resources.

Shown here are the mammals unique to South America. The giant Glyptodonts were relatives of the armadillo. Litopterns were a wide-spread group of early herbivores.

Litopterns

Glyptodonts

Invaders from the north

Many of the early South American mammals were marsupials. Their young were born at an early stage of development and nursed in a pouch, as with the kangaroo of today. Most mammals on the separate continent of North America were placentals – their young were born at a much later stage of development.

When North and South America became joined, the placental mammals invaded from the North, and many of the marsupials became extinct. This was because the placentals were more intelligent and their young competed more to survive. Other South American mammals, such as the Megatherium, became extinct only with the appearance of humans on the continent, a few thousand years ago.

Megatherium

Proterothere

Marsupial carnivores

Recognizable Ancestors

Many of the mammals of two million years ago would have been familiar to us today. There were antelope and deer, and an early modern horse, with its toes fused together to form a single hoof, appeared.

Pygmies and giants

One striking difference to a modern observer would be the size of these animals. In North America there were beavers as large as modern bears. In Asia there was a rhinoceros as tall as an elephant. At the same time, miniature forms could also be found on small islands. On Malta there were elephants 1m (3.3 ft) tall and an even smaller form of hippopotamus.

Early mankind

Another mammal was expanding and dominating the plains of Africa and Asia — Homo erectus, the first "true human" and our direct ancestor. Homo erectus was about 1.6m (5·2 ft) tall and hunted and traveled in groups. They used tools, sharpened stakes and sticks for killing, or for digging up roots. They also knew how to use and control fire — probably the most important discovery ever made by any mammal. With this weapon, the large animals could be driven over cliffs and into traps.

The outlines above compare the beavers, warthogs and hyenas of the past with their present-day relatives.

Giants of the Plains

About one million years ago, herds of the huge Imperial mammoth roamed the plains of North America. Adult bulls stood over 4m (13 ft) at the shoulder and were twice the weight of a modern elephant.

The La Brea Tar Pits

The La Brea Tar Pits, in California, are one of the most important sites for fossils ever discovered. They contained water, but beneath the water were deep pits of soft, sticky tar. Animals came to drink and were trapped. Many fossils of the Imperial mammoth and other creatures of the same era, such as the ground sloth Nothrotherium have been excavated from La Brea.

Nothrotherium

Imperial mammoth

The Ice Ages

The great ice sheets that cover the Earth at both the North and South Poles have extended and retreated more than once in the past million years. The mammals of the northern continents had to adapt to colder conditions to survive. The Woolly mammoth and Woolly rhinoceros both had thick insulating coats.

Mammoths and humans

The mammoths provided humans with meat and hides. Even the mammoth's bones were used to build temporary shelters when the tribes followed the grazing herds. Cave paintings depict the mammoth and other animals on which early human beings depended.

Perfect specimens of the Woolly mammoth have been dug up from the frozen ground in Siberia. Not only were the skeletons intact, but the flesh was good enough to eat!

The Most Successful Mammal

The early ancestors of human beings owed their success to greater intelligence and their ability to adapt to changes in their environment. By living in groups they reduced the threat from more powerful predators and they learned how to cooperate with one another in the hunt for food. Finally, their ability to use tools and their mastery of fire enabled them to dominate all other mammals. By building shelters and using animal hides as clothes, they were better able to cope with climatic changes.

Early humans found that they could adapt to conditions as different as the cold northern plains of Siberia and the hot, arid areas of southern Africa. Intelligence and adaptability made humans the most successful of all mammals.

From hunters to herders

For many thousands of years early humans followed the great herds of horses and other animals as they migrated north and south with the coming of summer and winter. Others caught fish in lakes or rivers, or in coastal waters. This diet of meat was supplemented by roots and fruits.

But, about nine thousand years ago, this pattern of life changed. Instead of being hunted, animals such as sheep and goats were herded. By protecting these animals from other predators, the herders were certain of a year-round food supply.

As they no longer needed to follow the herds, settled communities could be built. This led to the planting and cultivation of crops such as wheat and barley. Human beings could now control the environment in which they lived.

The earliest settled farming communities yet discovered existed about 7,000 years B.C.

Living Together

The dominance of human beings has led to the extinction of many species of mammals. Only those animals that have lived in close association with humans, or benefited them have flourished. Domesticated livestock such as sheep, goats, pigs and cattle exist in greater numbers than they would have if left in the wild. This similarly includes dogs, cats and horses.

There are other animals that benefit less directly. Permanent human communities provide a constant source of food for rats and mice which feed on refuse and food scraps. In recent years other mammals, such as foxes, have moved into towns and cities and adapted to the new environment.

The future of the mammals

In the past, species of mammals died out over thousands of years, probably because they were unable to adapt to the slowly changing climatic conditions. But in the past two to three hundred years, developments in human technology and the increase of human population have brought rapid and dramatic changes.

Some mammals have already become extinct, and many others are reduced to dangerously low numbers. In Kenya today, for example, only about 400 elephants remain. The future of the mammals is in our hands. By saving wild areas from agricultural development, and by caring for our natural resources, we may yet conserve the mammals that depend upon them.

Glossary

Carnivore A flesh-eating animal. The teeth of carnivores are suited to killing and slicing up their prey.

Evolution The theory of evolution tries to explain how animals change over thousands or millions of years. Those animals that are best suited to the environment are likely to survive and flourish. Animals that cannot adapt to changing conditions are more likely to die out.

Fossils The remains of animals and plants of the past preserved in rocks. Fossil remains tend to be of hard things like bones and teeth, but fossil imprints of plants and the feathers of early birds have been found.

Herbivore An animal that feeds only on plants. Herbivores have distinctive teeth for crushing, grinding and chewing tough vegetable matter.

Marsupials Marsupial young are born at a very early stage of development, and spend the first weeks and months of their lives suckled in a special pouch on the mother's body.

Placentals These are mammals that nurture their young for much longer periods of time in the mothers' bodies. Young placentals receive their food directly from their mothers' blood, through a special organ called the placenta. Placental mammals are born more fully developed than marsupials.

Index

PRINTED IN BELGIUM BY

proost
INTERNATIONAL BOOK PRODUCTION